FRANK
— N' —
GOAT

WRITTEN N' ILLUSTRATED
BY
JESSICA WATTS

Printed in the United States of America
First Printing, 2015
ISBN-13: 978-0692431467
Mighty Watts Publishing
www.FrankandGoat.com

No Frankensteins, monsters, or goats were harmed
in the writing of this book.

This, and all things, for Seth.

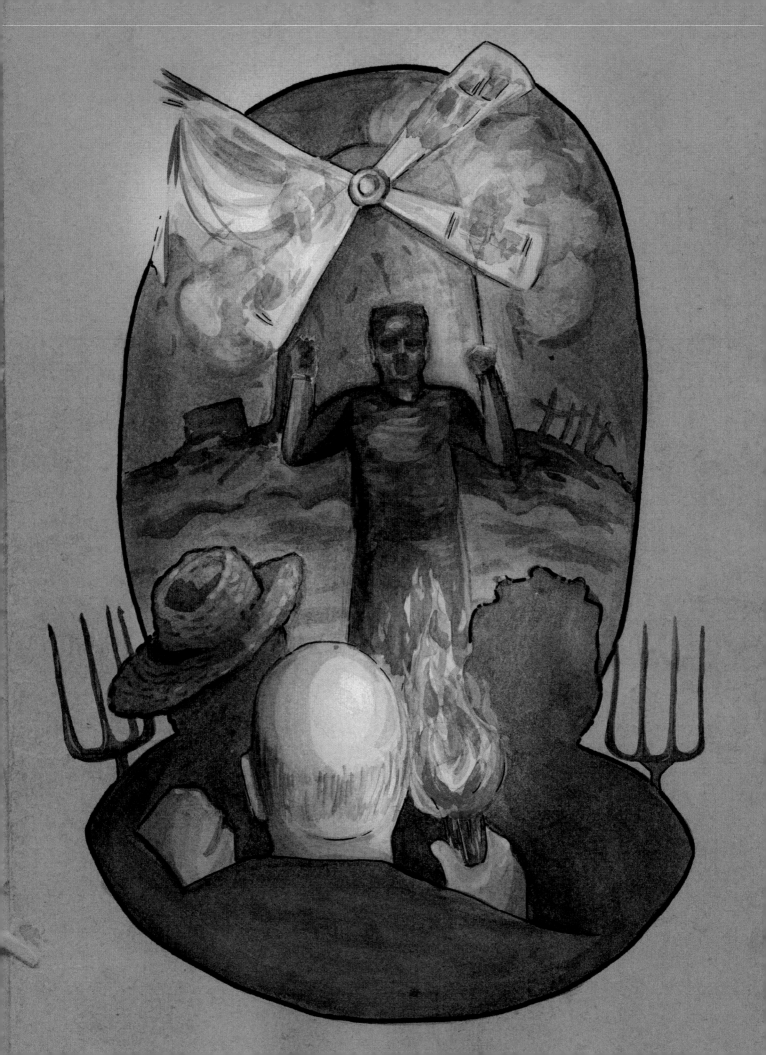

"... although the villagers burned the monster's lair to the ground, some say he escaped into the cold night. If you listen to the shadows, you may hear his sad shuffle — the sound of a creature doomed to wander the hard earth, rejected and alone, until the welcomed silence of death."

THE END

This is Goat.

He lacks aspirations and prospects.

He could also use a friend.

It was a day like any other. Goat was eating his weight in grass when he heard rustling. With a great groan, a monster staggered from the tall grass and dandelions, towering over the animal in terrifying fashion. Frank, as he was called, was expecting the usual reaction: "OH MY GOD! A MONSTER! HIDE THE BABIES! GRAB THE PITCHFORKS! DIEEE!"

But that fatty-pants Goat just kept on stuffing his four-chambered stomach. Few things come between a goat and lunch, and that includes half-dead, 8 foot tall monsters.

Pooped, the monster plopped down in the grass alongside the munching mammal. Frank let out a great sigh, and a tear rolled down his cadaverous cheek.

Why was he so blue (or rather, green)? Local villagers had chased him with pitchforks the night before, calling him names and shouting things like, "My god, a monster! Find your pointy objects!"

Frank couldn't understand how humans could be so cruel, just because he looked different - and because he was built from the corpses of their friends and neighbors. But that was hardly his fault! That's just the way he came into this world, borrowed toes, filched elbows and all.

Wiping away a tear, the meandering morgue sulked off to be alone with his sad thoughts. Goat, however, felt a stirring deep within his little goat heart. Being a herd animal, Goat didn't like being alone much. He followed the sulky stiff, wondering whether Frank had any snacks.

Frank needed to think. He went to a contemporary art museum, which is a favorite haunt for moody people. He started with the modern art... But he didn't get it. This reminded him of how people didn't get him, which made him sad all over again.

You may have heard that goats eat tin cans or garbage. That's a damn lie. They actually have quite refined palates. They are also not welcomed in museums.

The gloomy green giant decided to try watching a movie instead, to get his mind off of things. Goat invited himself along. It was then that Frank discovered they both shared a mutual love for monster flicks, or, as Frank called them, documentaries. Frank also appreciated that Goat didn't talk during the movie, or ever, for that matter. Because goats don't talk.

And so, day after day, the two creatures found themselves in each other's company. They shared similar opinions on the joys of not bathing, and of how scary fire can be. Despite their disagreements on the virtues of country music and head butting, their debates were as lively as their stench.

As their relationship continued to blossom, Frank realized he had made a friend! The adventurous twosome thrived, grabbing life by the horns...pun so, so, intended. They were regulars at Tuesday Trivia Night, competing as "Stitch Cassidy and The Sundance Kid." They even came in second place once.

Frank and Goat also found their fair share of trouble there since, as everyone knows, goats can't handle their liquor.

They were unstoppable. Goat encouraged Frank to forget his past and face his fear of making new friends... Lady friends. Goat also helped Frank make sure he didn't sound like a creep in his dating profile. Frank definitely needed that help.

"The most important thing about a potential partner?"

"Hopeless necromantic," typed Frank.

"Delete," hooved goat.

(If reading aloud, you should probably perform a long, contented sigh here.)

Who would have thought a corpse and a farm animal could make such a perfect pair? It felt like only yesterday the world was against Frank. But today, basking in the warm glow of the sun and friendship, he felt truly happy.

Their days were filled with possibility and joy. When watching his friend frolic and play, Frank forgot all about the trauma of his past.

That is, until Goat was struck by lightning.

Goat was killed instantly.

Frank was shocked and devastated, though not nearly as shocked as Goat. There his best friend lay, hoofs up. Goat had bought the farm. He also smelled delicious, which left Frank with some unsettling feelings.

Nothing is so painful as the sudden loss of a loved one. The agony of losing Goat stung even worse than the harsh words and pointy pitchforks of the angry mob. It was unexpected and incredibly unfair. It was almost as if some divine, book-writing power had just decided to smite Goat on a whim for some sort of literary climax.

Sadly, like Frank, we will all lose a best friend someday, though probably not to lightning. But don't despair! Take comfort, dear reader. Even though these sad days are unavoidable, we will always have happy memories of loved ones before they ascended to sing with that choir in the sky. While death is sadly inevitable, our grief will soon pass like a swallowed penny through one's bowels.

Painful change just takes time.

Or, if you're quite literal about the best friends forever thing, you can dig them up instead.

IT'S ALIVE! Frank brought Goat back from the dead!

Frank knew a thing or two about reanimation from personal experience. After borrowing some pieces from the pet cemetery, and some leftovers from the butcher's shop, Frank was able to improvise a pretty impressive science experiment. Despite decomposing just a few hours prior, Goat now looked rather fetching. In fact, the bolts Frank installed on Goat looked so cute that Frank considered adding some to his own neck.

Goat's tail did get lost somewhere along the way, though. But it wasn't anything a cat tail from the pet cemetery couldn't fix. Apologies to Garfield.

Embracing in undead devotion, Goat was deeply touched by the unrelenting love of his best friend and the lengths to which he had gone. Makes you wonder if your best friend would go through such tribulations to bring you back to life.

Just saying.

Everything was all crimson and clover again. The pulse-impaired pals set out to not only enjoy their second chance at life, but to experience their friendship all over again. New adventures awaited, and they were ready to live life to its fullest; after all, you only live once! Or twice.

As fate would have it, being undead brought them closer together than ever before. They now understood each other on an even deeper level. Goat could sympathize with Frank's complaints about his achy muscles (damn rigor mortis!), or how Halloween is the best holiday ever. Free candy for no reason? Awesome!

No matter where they went or what they did, life was grand. Like a thrift store coat, their friendship was just as fabulous the second time around.

I suppose now that we're at the end, you're looking for some sort of moral to this twisted tale? Perhaps you can leave with this: Don't fly kites in lightning storms, illustrated books take serious liberty with the laws of nature and science, and once you find a friend who means the world to you, do everything in your power to keep them in your afterlife.

ROCKY ROAD
ALMOND
CARAMEL
HONEY
ESPRESSO
LEMON
—— NUTS · SPRINKLES ——

And perhaps one day, you may have a friendship as happily-ever-afterly as that of Frank and Goat.

the End